CRAFT TOPICS

KNIGHTS

FACTS • THINGS TO MAKE • ACTIVITIES

RACHEL WRIGHT

Franklin Watts

London • New York • Sydney • Toronto

First published in Great Britain
in 1991 by
Franklin Watts
96 Leonard Street
London EC2A 4RH

First published in the USA by
Franklin Watts Inc
387 Park Avenue South
New York, N.Y. 10016

First published in Australia by
Franklin Watts
14 Mars Road
Lane Cove
NSW 2066

UK ISBN: 0 7496 0699 1

Editor: Hazel Poole
Text consultant: I. D. D. Eaves,
Keeper of Armour, Royal Armouries,
HM Tower of London
Designed by: Sally Boothroyd
Artwork by: Ed Dovey
A CIP catalogue record for this book
is available from the British Library

Printed in the United Kingdom

CONTENTS

EARLY KNIGHTS

Knights were armoured warriors, trained to fight on horseback. For much of the Middle Ages they dominated European life, both on and off the battlefield.

The Middle Ages is the name given to the period from about the 700s AD to 1500 AD. During this time Europe was often at war. Before mounted warriors arrived on the scene, most of the fighting had been done by untrained foot soldiers. Up until then, it had been almost impossible for a horseman to stay in the saddle and fight at the same time.

Between the late 700s and the 1100s, however, all this changed as western Europe saw four "inventions" come into general use. They were the stirrup, the nailed horse-shoe, the high-backed saddle and the heavier lance. Together, they turned the horseman into a formidable fighting force.

▲ A 12th century picture showing knights in shock combat.

With a steel-tipped wooden lance gripped firmly under his arm, and his body fixed to his horse by saddle and stirrups, a rider could hit his enemy with the full force of both himself and his charging horse — all without losing his balance. The age of the knight had begun.

KNIGHT KEEPING

Kings needed knights, but they couldn't afford to keep permanent armies of them. Providing for such an army in peacetime would have cost a small fortune. So, instead of paying wages, some kings agreed to give part of their land to their leading knights. In return, these knights had to promise to be loyal, to help the king fight his wars, and to keep law and order in their own parts of the country.

KING

BARONS

These leading knights then shared out their land amongst their own knightly followers, offering them a similar deal. In this way, high and low knights alike had land to live on and had control over the peasants who worked on that land. This whole arrangement — land for services — was later called feudalism. It turned many knights into wealthy and powerful mini rulers.

KNIGHTS

PEASANTS

Not all knights benefited from feudalism. Some remained landless, fighting for whomever would pay them. Others wandered the countryside in search of fame and fortune.

▲ *This pyramid shows how feudalism was structured. Everyone was expected to serve God and their social superiors. The workers on the bottom row had the roughest deal of all. Some of them were actually owned by their overlord.*

KNIGHTS OF GOD

The first knights were not necessarily nobles. They were simply men who could afford a horse. On the whole, they were rough and ready characters who earned a living by fighting. If there was no enemy about, they fought amongst themselves to show off their skills.

Their wild, unruly behaviour began to worry the Church. In those days, the Catholic Church was immensely powerful in Europe. So, when it pointed out that knights everywhere had a duty to fight for God, protect the poor and generally start behaving themselves, many sat up and listened.

CHIVALRY

During the 1100s, the knights went one step further and developed their own code of behaviour, which the Church then sponsored. This code of behaviour, called chivalry, demanded that a knight "live pure, speak true, right wrong, [and] follow [the Christ], the King".* Later on, it also expected the perfect knight to fight on behalf of a lady, as this was supposed to inspire him to greater bravery.

Needless to say, all this was more easily said than done, and some knights did not live up to the chivalrous ideal.

Chivalry and the Church's backing made knighthood glamorous — an honour valued by lords and kings. As a result, knights became a part of the nobility, a class of warrior aristocrats. Snobbery set

in and, before long, most new knights were the sons of knights rather than of poor men.

*Lord Tennyson, The Idylls of the King (Gareth and Lynette, l. 1 1 7).
A young lady offers her heart to the knight she has chosen as her champion. ▼*

BRASS PORTRAITS

Detailed engravings of knights in armour can sometimes be found in old churches. These portraits, made of a mixture of metals similar to brass, are often set into the floor. If you find one, why not ask permission to make a rubbing of it?

You will need: a duster • a piece of brass rubbing paper and wax (both can be bought from art shops or brass rubbing centres) • masking tape.

1. Dust the brass and cover it with paper. Use strips of masking tape to hold the paper in place.

2. Smooth the paper with your fingertips until a faint outline of the knight appears. Hold a wax crayon lengthwise and gently rub it up and down within this outline.

3. When you have a clear image of the knight, start rubbing much harder. Use different coloured wax to highlight details.

4. When rubbing the edges or fiddly parts of the brass, it helps if you hold your wax like an ordinary crayon.

5. When you have finished, peel off the masking tape and mount your rubbing on to a piece of card.

DRESSED TO KILL

After the first thunderous charge into battle, a knight's lance was useless. So he dropped it and fought with his main weapon, his sword. During the second half of the 1300s, however, it became common for a knight to carry a short axe or mace (knobbed or spiked club) as well.

MAIL MEN

The first knights wore hauberks — long shirts made from small, interlinking metal rings. They also wore open-faced iron helmets, and carried round shields.

By 1100, mounted knights were carrying kite-shaped shields, which protected their legs much better than the round shields had done.

By the 1200s, a knight bound for battle would have been dressed as shown opposite.

▲ This 13th century picture shows three knightly weapons in action – the sword, the axe and the mace. The worried looking man on the left is trying to fire a giant catapult called a trebuchet.

8

padded cap

fabric shirt

aketon
(This was a padded coat which stopped the hauberk from bruising the knight's skin.)

breeches
(Linen or woollen stockings were worn underneath these.)

coif

Great helm
(This would have been hot and heavy to wear.)

heater shield

mail leggings
(They were attached by laces to a belt.)

hauberk
(Rusty hauberks were cleaned by being tossed about in a bag containing sand and vinegar.)

linen (or other fabric) surcoat
(A surcoat helped to keep the knight cool when fighting in the sun.)

mail mittens
(These were usually part of the hauberk's sleeves.)

spurs

Although knights kept their armour spotless, they weren't so keen on keeping themselves clean. Until the 1200s, most of them didn't bathe because they thought it sapped their strength.

9

Metal Lobsters

By 1300, armour makers had learnt to re-inforce parts of mail armour with iron plates. By 1400, they had perfected this technique and were putting together complete suits of made-to-measure steel plated armour. Made of about 200 plates which were joined together to make 12 or more main pieces, this armour was often strapped or laced to a knight's body.

A knight certainly welcomed his squire's help when putting on his armour. ▼

The steel plates used were skilfully shaped in such a way that weapons would skid off them.

Arranged rather like a lobster shell, most of these plates overlapped each other in order to leave as few gaps as possible. Since the plates were joined to each other by smaller plates, held together by sliding rivets, the armour was fairly easy to move in. Where there had to be gaps to allow for even more movement, a knight was protected by the mail he wore underneath.

In all, a suit of plate armour, called a harness, weighed about 40 to 60lbs. Yet, because this weight was spread evenly over a knight's body, it wasn't unbearable. In fact, one French knight proved the point by leaping on to a horse, turning a somersault and climbing the underside of a ladder — all in full armour!

MAKE A KNIGHT'S HELMET

You will need: stiff paper or thin card • scissors or a craft knife • glue • sticking tape • paint • paintbrush • pencil • coloured paper.

3. Paint your helmet and tape it together at the back.

▲ **1.** Cut out a piece of stiff paper which will fit right around your head. Cut and fold tabs along the top.

▲ **2.** Hold the paper against your face and mark two slits for your eyes. Cut these eye slits out. Don't forget to cut breathing holes too!

▲ **4.** To make a plume, draw a line across a sheet of coloured paper, about 5cm from one edge. Cut strips up to this line. Roll the paper into a tube and tape it together.

5. Cut out a stiff paper circle for the top of your helmet and paint it. Make a hole in its centre, push the plume through and secure it with tape.

6. Now glue your helmet together and prepare for battle!

Although this home-made helmet looks better with a plume, knights of old would have worn this type of helmet without one.

COATS OF ARMS

Chief

Fess

Pale

Bar

Bend

Saltire

Chevron

Pile

Cross

12

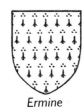
Vair

Ermine

In the heat of battle, one knight in mail looked very like another. Therefore, to make it easier to tell friend from foe, knights had their own personal patterns or emblems painted on to their shields. These emblems, which were sometimes embroidered on to their surcoats, became known as "coats of arms".

Before long, many rich families had their own individual coat of arms, which was passed down from parent to child. Women displayed their father's or husband's arms on their personal possessions, and many wives combined the two, creating a new coat of arms.

The surface of a knight's shield was called the field. The figures or shapes on it were called charges. The simplest charges were chief, fess, pale, bar, bend, saltire, chevron, pile, cross.

The field and charges had to be painted in certain colours. Only red, black, blue, green, purple, gold and silver were allowed.

Furs, patterns which looked like animal skins, were also used. The two most common ones were vair and ermine.

To ensure that each design was easy to identify, colour was never placed on colour; nor metal on metal; nor fur on fur.

You can see coats of arms in many different places — on park gates, pillar boxes, school crests and stained-glass windows.

▲ *A husband's and wife's shields were sometimes combined like this to create a new coat of arms.*

▲ *These shields were drawn in about 1244 by Matthew Paris. He was a learned monk and historian from St. Albans, England.*

MAKE A STAINED-GLASS WINDOW

Design a coat of arms for you and your family. Your charges could show what your mum and dad do, or what your own hobbies are. Keep your design fairly simple as you need crayons for this project and they are not good for drawing tiny details.

You will need: white paper • pencil • crayons • cotton wool • vegetable oil.

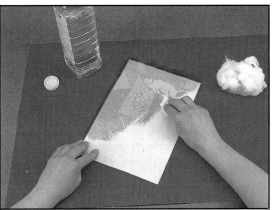

▲ **3.** Pour a little vegetable oil on to a ball of cotton wool and wipe it over the back of your design.

4. When the paper is dry, stick it on a windowpane. Your coat of arms will glow when the sun shines through it, just like a stained-glass window.

▲ **1.** Draw your design on a piece of white paper and then go over its outlines in black crayon. You'll need to press quite hard.

2. Colour the spaces between the black lines. Make sure that the paper shows through only where you particularly want it to.

Knights in Waiting

The first knighting ceremonies were very simple. After serving an apprenticeship, a would-be knight was awarded his sword and spurs by an older knight, and that was that. In time, however, both the training and the ceremony became much more complicated.

A boy of noble birth, destined to become a knight, left home at the age of 7. He was sent to a great lord's castle, where he was taught to handle horses and weapons and to be polite. In return, he had to run errands.

▲A quintain was used for lance practice. The squire had to hit the shield on the crossbar and duck before the sandbag on the other end of the crossbar swung round and hit him.

When he was about 14 years old, he became a squire. This meant that he was now the personal servant of a knight.

A squire had to look after his master and follow him wherever he went — even into battle. If a knight got into difficulties on the battlefield, his squire came to his rescue. If he got hurt, his squire helped him to safety and dressed his wounds. If he was killed, his squire made sure that he was buried properly.

Away from the battlefield, a squire spent hours getting used to wearing armour and improving his fighting skills.

A squire's life wasn't all war and chores, though. He practised other important knightly pursuits, such as singing, dancing and entertaining the ladies.

When he was about 21, a squire who could afford his own armour and horse was ready to become a knight. In preparation he had to have a bath, to wash away his sins. After bathing, he put on clean clothes — a red robe, to signify the blood he would shed for God, and black stockings, to remind him of death. He then spent the night praying in a castle's chapel.

His moment of glory came the next day when, after a church service, he joined other squires gathered outside. In front of an excited crowd, he stepped forward to receive his sword and golden spurs. He then knelt before a senior knight who solemnly tapped him with a sword on the neck or shoulders. At last, his years of training were over. He had become a knight.

Sometimes a squire showed such bravery in war that he was knighted on the battlefield. ▼

FIGHTING FOR FUN

When knights weren't fighting wars, they would play war games! By 1100, mock battles, called tournaments or tourneys, were popular in most parts of northern Europe. Two teams of knights would spend an afternoon battering one another. The winners were those left upright at the end of the game!

As in a real war, knights tried to capture their opponents rather than kill them. Successful knights did well from the ransoms paid for captured opponents.

RULES AND REFEREES

The early tourneys had few rules and no referees. They were more like riots than sport, with players getting hurt and killed.

Later tourneys were slightly more civilised. Rules, referees and blunted weapons were introduced, and the war games themselves became part of a great carnival of chivalry.

BANS

Although tourneys were excellent training for war, ?? ??ch was shocked by their brut?? ??ried to ban them. Various ?? ?? curb them too, becau?? ??ged scheming rebels to gat?? ?? Yet, despite such fierce op?? ??e knights refused to give ?? ?? d continued fighting each other for fun.

BATTLE FOR TWO

Mock battles were popular, but jousting became even more so. The joust was a contest between two mounted knights, armed with lances. Each knight had to try to break his lance against his

opponent, without hitting him below the belt. Sometimes the knights would finish their fight on foot, using either swords or poleaxes.

GAMES OF WAR

If there was a lull in a battle or a boring wait during a siege, knights from the two opposing armies might meet for a tourney. Once their game was over, they would return to their respective camps and wait for the real war to start again.

▶ A scene from a joust at St. Inglevert in France, taken from a 15th century copy of a chronicle about tourneying.

STAGE YOUR OWN JOUST

▲ **3.** Cover the stand with tissue paper. Make drapes by pleating strips of tissue paper and gluing them into position. Decorate the drapes with the foil sweet wrappers.

4. Paint spectators on some thin card. Cut them out and stick them to the inside of the stand's window.

5. Add thin card supports, painted to look like wood, and glue the completed stand into place. Make more stands in the same way.

▲ **1.** Turn a large cardboard box on to one of its sides and cut away the top. Make deep cuts into the two remaining sides so that they open out slightly. Now paint the inside of the box.

▲ **2.** To build a stand, cut down a smaller box to the size you want it. Stand it on its cut-away end and make a window in the front.

▲ **6.** Draw and then paint a charging knight on to thick card. Cut him out, leaving a long strip attached to his horse's back legs. Now make a second knight riding in the opposite direction.

▲ **7.** Cut a narrow slit into each side of your painted box and slot the knights into them.

▲ **8.** To avoid collisions, jousters in the second half of the 1400s were separated by a wooden barrier called a tilt.

To make a tilt, cut a strip of thick card, slightly longer than the width of your box. Paint it and add a tab to each end. Coat the tabs with glue and stick the tilt between the knights.

HOLY WARS

In 1095, the Catholic Church made a dramatic plea, calling on knights everywhere to defend their Christian faith.

A group of Muslims had seized Jerusalem and were stopping Christians from visiting the city. As Jesus had lived in and around Jerusalem, Christians saw these areas as their Holy Land and wanted everybody else out.

HEADING FOR THE HOLY LAND

Knights quickly rallied to the Church's call and set off on the first of their crusades. "Crusade" simply means "war of the cross". Once in the Holy Land, the crusaders fought furiously and captured Jerusalem. They set up four states of their own and built huge castles to protect themselves. However, keeping the Muslims at bay was hard work, which is why, during the 1100s, new knightly orders were founded to defend the crusading states.

◄Crusaders occasionally used their enemies' severed heads as missiles.

WARRIOR MONKS

The Templars, the Knights of St. John, and the Teutonic Knights were the three most important new orders. Their members were disciplined fighters who had vowed to live simply, worship God, and remain unmarried. The only trouble was that as each order grew richer, some members conveniently forgot their vows!

Feared and envied by European rulers, many Templars were burnt to death after the crusades, and in 1313 their order was disbanded. The other orders fared better, and ended up doing their Christian work both in Europe and abroad.

Yet, in spite of their failings, it was largely due to these orders that the Christians managed to hold on to the Holy Land until 1291.

RICHES FROM THE EAST

Many crusaders profited from their stay in the Holy Land. They learnt how to make paper, windmills and carpets. They later returned to Europe, armed with silks, velvets, dyes, mirrors, apricots, rice and melons, as well as new ideas about astronomy and maths. If nothing else, the crusades gave knights knowledge and luxuries they had not known before.

The three main military orders set up to defend the Holy Land at the time of the crusades. ▼

The Templars (c. 1170)

The Knights of St. John (c. 1250)

The Teutonic Knights (c. 1280)

The Templars were founded in the early 1100s. Their job was to care for pilgrims and to protect the Holy Sepulchre where Jesus was buried.

The main mission of the Order of St. John was to care for poor and sick pilgrims visiting the Holy Land. It became a military Order at the time of the first crusades.

The Order of Teutonic Knights was set up in 1190. The Order was German in origin and its early work involved helping German pilgrims in the Holy Land.

Krak des Chevaliers, in Syria. Crusaders also learnt something about castle-building from the Arabs. ▶

Fortress Homes

Few knights owned castles, but many lived in them.

STICKS AND STONES

The first castles were made of wood. They were later replaced by much larger stone castles, surrounded by thick stone walls. These new castles were like tiny towns, with tailors, priests and bakers all working within their walls.

UNDER ATTACK

Castles were fortresses as well as homes. Where possible, they were built on or near natural defences such as hills and rivers. Even so, an uninvited army could still force its way into them.

Attackers sometimes tried to starve their enemy into surrender by camping outside the castle and stopping all food deliveries. This was called mounting a siege. However, if the castle was well-stocked, a siege could drag on for months. This deterred many attackers who couldn't afford to leave their own homes unguarded for so long.

Those who preferred a quicker form of attack often tried to storm their way in instead. Using giant catapults, they hurled rocks at or over the castle walls, and tried to smash down the gate with a battering ram.

While these assaults were going on above ground, fellow attackers might be busy tunnelling beneath the castle walls. When they had finished, they burnt the wooden props used to support the tunnel's roof and waited for the wall to collapse.

Some knights refused to dirty their hands tunnelling and only took part in hand-to-hand combat. They considered all other forms of warfare most unknightly!

CLIMBING THE WALLS

Attackers often tried to take a castle by direct assault, too. Dodging arrows, rocks and boiling water fired down from above, they would rush to scale the walls. Some would use ladders, while others climbed tall wooden siege towers which were wheeled up against the castle wall.

The catapults to the left of the castle are trebuchets. The catapult with a spoon-like arm is a mangonel. Both could hurl heavy missiles, but the trebuchet was the more accurate of the two. ▼

SUPER CASTLES

As the Middle Ages progressed, European castles gradually improved. More outer walls were added, moats were dug to stop tunnelling, and gatehouses were built to defend the castle's entrance. Until the 1400s, when cannons became popular, these castles were almost impossible to attack successfully.

▲ Caerphilly Castle, Wales.

23

CARDBOARD CASTLES

The main tower of the early stone castles was called the keep. This was where the castle's lord and his knights ate and slept.

TO MAKE A KEEP

▲ **I.** Cut evenly spaced notches along the top of a large square cardboard box. Cut deeper notches at each corner and cover the box with card.

▲ *Rochester Castle, Kent, England*

TO MAKE A TOWER FOR THE KEEP

▲ **2.** Cut out a piece of card. It should be slightly taller than the keep, but the same width.

▲ **3.** Fold the card lengthwise into four with a tab at one end. Open it out again.

4. Cut arrow slits into the two centre panels so that castle defenders can fire out, but enemy archers can't shoot in.

5. Make battlements by cutting evenly spaced notches along the top of the tower. Use a craft knife to cut arrow slits into the higher parts of your battlements.

▲ **6.** Decorate the tower and paint doors near the top of each of its outer panels. Check that the base of each door starts below the keep's battlements, when the tower is in place.

TO MAKE THE TOWER'S ROOF

▲ **7.** Measure the width of one of your tower's panels. Draw a square with sides this same length.

8. Paint the square, add four tabs and cut the whole shape out.

▲ **9.** Cover all four tabs with glue and fold the tower around its roof. Now glue the side of the tower.

▲ **10.** Rest the tower on a corner of the keep, with its glued panels facing inwards. Mark the tower where it touches the keep. Using these marks as guide lines, make two long cuts and slot the tower into place. If the tower looks crooked, trim the bottom of its two inner panels.

11. Make three more towers for your keep in the same way.

12. Finally, stick a paper flag on to shortened straws and glue the straws to each tower's roof.

Stone keeps had rampart walks so that their soldiers could get from one tower to another.

TO MAKE RAMPART WALKS

13. Cut out a rectangle of card, long enough to fit between two towers.

▲ **14.** Fold the card as shown and cover the two tabs with glue.

▲ **15.** Stick the two tabs to the keep, just below the battlements. Repeat this until you have four walkways joining your towers.

16. When your keep and walkways are complete, paint them.

TO MAKE CURTAIN WALLS

▲ **17.** Cut notches along the top of painted strips of card. Don't forget to cut arrow slits too. Position the strips around your keep, sticking them together where necessary. Where your wall bends into a corner, cut off a couple of the notches.

▲ **18.** Make wall towers in the same way that you made the towers for your keep and slot them into the corners of your curtain wall. Glue rampart walks to each wall.

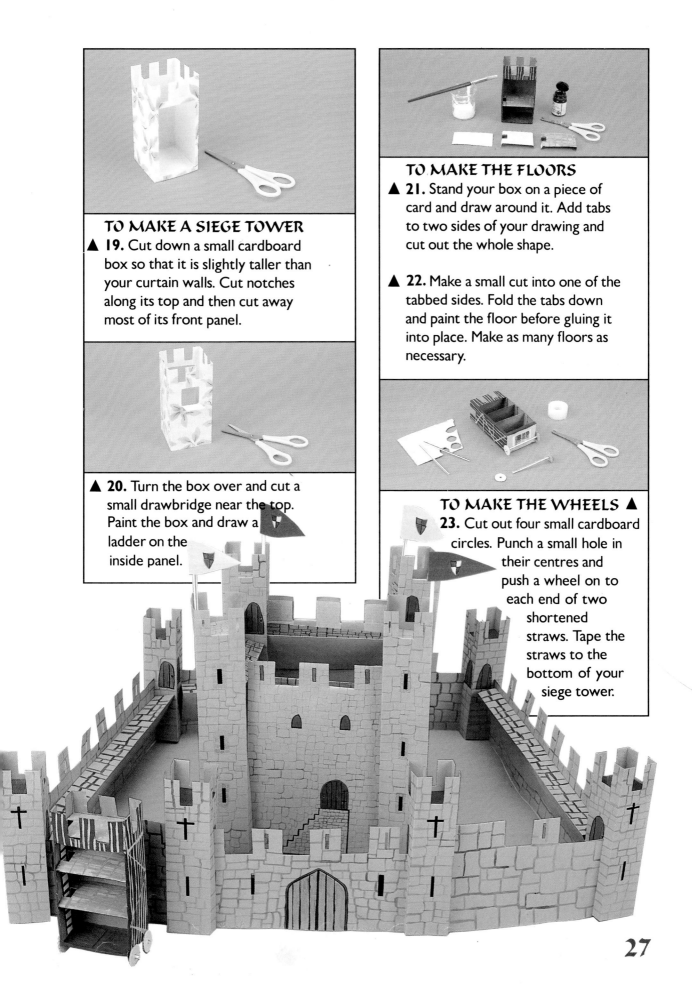

TO MAKE A SIEGE TOWER

▲ **19.** Cut down a small cardboard box so that it is slightly taller than your curtain walls. Cut notches along its top and then cut away most of its front panel.

▲ **20.** Turn the box over and cut a small drawbridge near the top. Paint the box and draw a ladder on the inside panel.

TO MAKE THE FLOORS

▲ **21.** Stand your box on a piece of card and draw around it. Add tabs to two sides of your drawing and cut out the whole shape.

▲ **22.** Make a small cut into one of the tabbed sides. Fold the tabs down and paint the floor before gluing it into place. Make as many floors as necessary.

TO MAKE THE WHEELS ▲

23. Cut out four small cardboard circles. Punch a small hole in their centres and push a wheel on to each end of two shortened straws. Tape the straws to the bottom of your siege tower.

KNIGHTLY FRIEZE

The Bayeux Tapestry is probably the most famous piece of embroidery in the world. 70 metres long, it shows the events leading up to William the Conqueror's invasion of England in 1066.

Using the Bayeux Tapestry for inspiration, why not make a fabric frieze? It could show a day in the life of a knight or the story of a spectacular battle.

1. To make your cloth background very firm, glue a piece of thick card on to the back of your length of material.

2. Draw your designs on tracing paper and trace them on to some fabric. Cut out your fabric shapes and arrange them on a cloth background before sticking them down.

You will need: tracing paper • pencil • a length of rayon or calico for the background • a piece of thick card • sharp scissors • white PVA glue • glue brush • cocktail sticks for spreading tiny amounts of glue • fabric scraps • ribbons • wools • threads • sequins, etc.

3. Try fraying, pleating, plaiting, and overlapping fabrics to create different effects. Add extra detail using ribbon, thread, buttons and beads.

THE END OF THE KNIGHT

By the 1200s, feudalism had started to crumble and leading knights no longer had to fight for the king. Instead, they gave him money to hire soldiers to take their place.

The times were gradually changing in other ways, too. Europe started to become more peaceful, and trade began to boom. Successful merchants and traders found that they could now buy their way into the nobility. The knightly class was no longer as select as it had once been.

FOOTMEN v CAVALRYMEN

Things were looking bad for knights . . . and getting worse. By the 1500s, long bows, hand guns and cannons had all become common weaponry, and the old-fashioned knight was clearly no match for any of them.

Foot soldiers, called pikemen, had also arrived to stay. Standing in closely packed ranks, holding pikes of up to six metres long in front of them, these pikemen could easily skewer a stampede of charging knights. The age of the knight had finally come to an end.

Some orders of knighthood which were founded in the Middle Ages still exist today. The Order of the Garter is one of them. ▼

Glossary

Aristocrat — a member of the nobility or a privileged class.

Astronomy — the study of stars, planets, comets, etc.

Battering ram — a tree trunk or giant wooden pole, often fitted with an iron tip, which was swung to and fro against a castle wall or gate to smash it down.

Battlement — a line of notches along the top of a wall or tower. Soldiers leaned over the gaps, called crenels, to fire at the enemy below, and took cover behind the higher parts of the wall, called merlons.

Crusades — or Wars of the Cross, were religious wars, fought by Christians to win back the Holy Land from the Muslims.

Curtain wall — the wall around a castle.

Faith — religious belief.

Fortress — a place built to resist attack.

Gatehouse — a tower built over a castle's main gates. The gatehouse was the best defended part of a castle.

Holy Land — modern-day Israel, Jordan, Lebanon and Syria. This is the part of the world where Jesus lived and taught.

Lance — long, tapering wooden pole with a metal tip. After about 1100, it became common for knights to charge at their enemy with a lance gripped rigidly under their right armpit.

Longbow — a wooden bow, about the same height as a man.

Moat — a deep trench which was dug around a castle and filled with water.

Muslim — someone who follows the Islamic religion.

Orders — communities of monks or nuns who follow a strict religious way of life. The Templars, the Knights of St. John, and the Teutonic Knights were military orders whose members were supposed to live like monks.

Orders of Knighthood (Orders of Chivalry) — There have been many orders of Knighthood set up over the centuries. Although they may have started up for different reasons, each order was like an exclusive knight club for the rich and famous. Members promised to support one another at all times, to obey their Grand Master and to do knightly deeds. Unlike monastic orders, such as the Templars, these orders of Knighthood did not vow to live like monks.

Poleaxe — an axe with a heavy head ("poll"), set on a one to two metre wooden pole.

Ransom — goods or money demanded for the release of a prisoner.

Squire — a trainee knight.

Vow — a solemn promise.

RESOURCES

BOOKS
Fiction
Sir Cedric by Roy Gerrard (Victor Gollancz).

The Cat and the Devil by James Joyce (Moonlight Publishing). Amusing story set in the Middle Ages.

The Road to Camlann by Rosemary Sutcliff (Knight's Books, Hodder and Stoughton).

Knight's Fee by Rosemary Sutcliff (Red Fox).

The Story of King Arthur (Kingfisher Books). Re-telling of the Arthurian legends by Robin Lister.

Robin Hood by Sarah Hayes and Patrick Benson (Walker Books). A famous adventure story set in the Middle Ages.

Non fiction
The Time Traveller Book of Knights and Castles by Judy Hindley (Usborne).

Knights and Castles by Jonathon Rutland (Kingfisher).

Living in Castle Times by Robin Gee (Usborne).

See Inside a Castle ed. R J Unstead (Kingfisher).

Kings, Barons and Serfs by R J Unstead (Macdonald).

SOFTWARE
Rickitt Educational Media supply a wide range of relevant software for 8 years +, including *Castle Under Attack* – a strategy game for two or more players and *Lancelot* – an adventure which recreates the knightly age.

For further details contact:
Rickitt Educational Media,
Ilton, Ilminster, Somerset TA19 9BA.

PLACES TO VISIT
There are various collections of arms and armour in the British Isles. Your local tourist board will be able to tell you which is your nearest.

Britain's national collection of armour is kept at:
The Royal Armouries,
HM Tower of London,
Tower Hill, London EC3N 4AB.
Tel: 071-709 0765.

Similarly, there are a number of castles and medieval buildings open to the public. The following addresses will help you to track down what you're looking for:

Cadw: Welsh Historic Monuments,
Brunel House, Fitzalan Road,
Cardiff CF2 1UY.
Tel: (0222) 465511.

The National Trust for Scotland,
5 Charlotte Square, Edinburgh.

The National Trust,
36 Queen Anne's Gate, London
SW1H 9AS.

Northern Ireland Tourist Board,
River House,
48 High Street, Belfast BT1 2DS.
Tel: 0232 246609.

DEMONSTRATIONS
The British Jousting Centre and Belvoir Castle host medieval jousting tournaments. For further information and dates contact:

Joan Diamond
British Jousting Centre
Tapely Park, Instow, Nr Bideford
North Devon EX39 4NT
Tel: Instow 861200

Belvoir Castle
Grantham, Lincs NG31 6BR
Tel: Grantham 870262

INDEX